PEOPLE OF THE
NORTHWEST
& SUBARCTIC

by
LINDA THOMPSON

Rourke
Publishing LLC
Vero Beach, Florida 32964

www.rourkepublishing.com

PHOTO CREDITS:
Library of Congress, Prints & Photographs Division, Edward S. Curtis Collection: cover, title page, pages 1, 7, 18, 20, 22, 24, 26-31, 34, 36, 37, 40, 43; Courtesy of the Alaska Department of Tourism: pages 5, 12, 25; Courtesy of The Division of Anthropology, American Museum of Natural History (AMNH): pages 6, 8, 12, 14, 18, 19, 21, 23, 25, 27, 40, 42; Courtesy of Mike Chowla: pages 6, 9; Courtesy of the National Anthropological Archives, Smithsonian Institution Museum: pages 9, 32, 38; Courtesy of Museum of History & Industry, Seattle: page 11; Museum of Anthropology at the University of British Colombia: page 14; Courtesy Charles Reasoner: pages 17, 23; Courtesy of the U.S. Fish & Wildlife Service: pages 17, 29.

DESIGN AND LAYOUT by Rohm Padilla, Mi Casa Publications, printing@taosnet.com

Library of Congress Cataloging-In-Publication Data

Thompson, Linda, 1941-
  People of the Northwest and subarctic / by Linda Thompson.
      p. cm. -- (Native peoples, Native lands)
Includes bibliographical references and index.
Contents: The northwest coast people today -- Where they came from --
Life on the northwest coast -- What they believe -- The artic and
subarctic peoples.
  ISBN 1-58952-756-9 (hardcover)
  1. Indians of North America--979 of North America--History--Juvenile
literature. 2. Indians of North America--Northwest Coast of North
America--Social life and customs--Juvenile literature. [1. Indians of
North America--Northwest Coast of North America.] I. Title. II.
Series: Thompson, Linda, 1941- Native peoples, Native lands.
  E78.N78T46 2003
  979.5004'97--dc21
                              2003011536

Printed in the U.S.A.

TITLE PAGE IMAGE:
Cowichan girl, a maiden of noble birth clad in goat-hair robe; photo by Edward S. Curtis.

TABLE OF CONTENTS

Tolfino Inlet,
Vancouver Island,
British Columbia,
Canada

Chapter I:

THE NORTHWEST COAST PEOPLE

*T*he Northwest Coast People descended from about a hundred **Native American** tribes (sometimes called **American Indians**) who lived in this region about 10,000 years ago. They spoke languages belonging to at least five different **language families**. The Northwest Coast includes the western coastal zone of present-day Washington, Oregon, and British Columbia, eastward to the Cascade Mountains. Yukutat Bay, Alaska, is the northern border.

**Waterfall on Vancouver Island,
British Columbia, Canada**

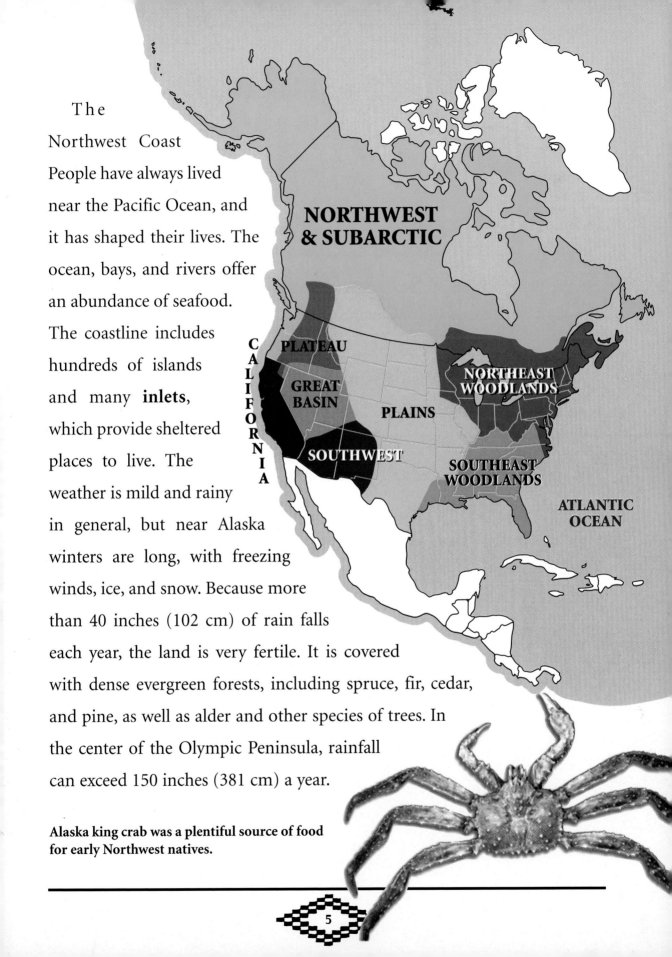

The Northwest Coast People have always lived near the Pacific Ocean, and it has shaped their lives. The ocean, bays, and rivers offer an abundance of seafood. The coastline includes hundreds of islands and many **inlets**, which provide sheltered places to live. The weather is mild and rainy in general, but near Alaska winters are long, with freezing winds, ice, and snow. Because more than 40 inches (102 cm) of rain falls each year, the land is very fertile. It is covered with dense evergreen forests, including spruce, fir, cedar, and pine, as well as alder and other species of trees. In the center of the Olympic Peninsula, rainfall can exceed 150 inches (381 cm) a year.

Alaska king crab was a plentiful source of food for early Northwest natives.

Sealskin pouch

The arrival of Christopher Columbus near what is now Florida in 1492 began a long process of European exploration and settlement of the "New World." But nearly three centuries passed before the Northwest Coast People felt that impact. In 1592, the first European, Juan de Fuca, sailed into this region. He was a Greek navigator sailing under the flag of Spain. The Straits of Juan de Fuca between Canada and the United States bear his name.

In 1741, Russian fur traders discovered that the Aleutian Islands teemed with sea otter colonies. Perhaps 20,000 Aleut, an Arctic People, lived among these islands and excelled at hunting sea otter. The Chinese valued the dense, shiny otter pelts for robes and capes and would pay hundreds of dollars for each pelt. To profit by this market, the Russians began forcing the Aleut to hunt for them. They whipped and threatened the men by capturing their wives and children as hostages. They also kidnapped Aleut women and children and sold them as slaves in Russia or China. This went on for more than 40 years, causing the Aleut population to fall to barely more than 2,000.

Straits of Juan de Fuca
photo by Mike Chowla

In 1802, Russian traders encountered the Tlingit [ta-ling-git], meaning "people" or "humans," living in what is now southeast Alaska. This group of well-organized Natives was better equipped to resist. They had obtained guns and gunpowder from English and American ship captains. They burned a Russian Fort on Sitka Island, capturing 3,000 sea otter pelts. Although Russia rebuilt the fort, the Tlingit were never subdued.

Beginning in the 1750s, England's **Northwest Company** and **Hudson's Bay Company** also sent traders into this region. They were looking for Natives to supply animal pelts. They also were interested in woodcarvings, baskets, and other objects that the Natives made. They were astonished to see 200-foot (61 m) long cedar

Sea lion

houses lined up along the beaches. The houses were carved and painted with animals and symbols of each Native **clan**.

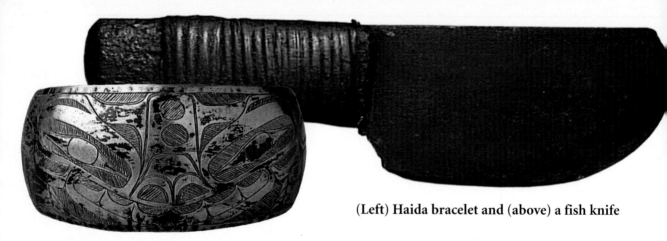

(Left) Haida bracelet and (above) a fish knife

In 1778, an English captain, James Cook, reached Vancouver Island. Misunderstanding the name of the Yuquot [yu-kwat] People, he called them "Nootka." British and American crews soon came in numbers, seeking pelts. During the 1790s, they sold more than 100,000 sea otter pelts in China. By 1820, very few sea otters were left, and the fur trade had shifted to land animals such as mink and beaver.

European traders also encountered the Haida in the Queen Charlotte Islands, which Natives called Haida Gwaii ("home of the people"). The Haida were happy to trade pelts for iron goods such as tools and utensils. Unaware of the pelts' value, they traded thousands of

Haida plate made of argillite

otter pelts for much less costly cloth, alcohol, muskets, and woolen blankets. As otter became scarce, they learned to make other items for trade. For example, they carved a soft black rock called **argillite**, which occurs only on Haida Gwai, into platters and decorative objects.

Europeans were also exploring the southern part of this region. By 1774, Spain had sent ships to present-day Oregon. In 1792, Captain George Vancouver of England sailed into the Straits of Juan de Fuca and glimpsed a tall, snow-covered mountain to the east. The Nisqually [nis-kwali] called this mountain Tahoma ("the mountain that is God"). Vancouver named it Mount Rainier, after a friend. He sent Peter Puget to explore the large body of water that Salish-speaking Natives called "Whulge" [hwulj]. Vancouver named it Puget Sound.

In 1806, the Lewis and Clark Expedition reached the mouth of the Columbia River, which divides the present states of Washington and Oregon. They met many Northwest Coast Natives along this stretch of the river, including several bands of Chinook [shin-uk].

Member of the Chinook people

Mount Rainier, Washington; photo by Mike Chowla

Nugget of gold

In general, Natives were friendly to these early explorers. But Europeans brought more than just blankets and metal. They brought diseases such as smallpox and measles, which severely affected Northwest Coast populations. Because Natives had no immunity to these diseases, thousands became ill and died.

In 1848, the Oregon Territory was created and settlers began to move west on the **Oregon Trail**. The Oregon Donation Land Act of 1850 gave 320 acres (129.5 ha) to each European settler over 18 years old. In the 1850s, miners began flocking to new gold discovery sites in southwestern Oregon, causing conflicts with Rogue [roag] and Umpqua [ump-kwa] Natives living in those areas.

This area was the western end of the Oregon Trail in the late 1800s. Today it is the Ankeny National Wildlife Refuge in Dallas, Oregon.

Chief
Seattle

Chief Seattle

Chief Seattle (1786-1866) was born near Puget Sound to a Suquamish father and a Duwamish mother. He learned to use firearms and took part in defensive raids against other tribes. The young warrior earned the name See-yahtlh [see-at-ul] after a successful raid against the Green River tribes. Soon, he was made chief of the Suquamish and Duwamish. In 1850, to honor him, David Maynard, an Indian agent and friend, changed the name of a town called Duwamps to "Seattle."

Chief Seattle tried all of his life to make the government keep its promises to Native tribes. He is famous for the words he spoke on many occasions. In 1854, he said: "Our God, the Great Spirit, seems to have forsaken us. Your God makes your people wax strong every day. Soon they will fill the land. Our people are ebbing away like a rapidly receding tide that will never return... How then can we be brothers? How can your God become our God and renew our prosperity and awaken in us dreams of returning greatness?"

Although **treaties** were made that protected Native rights, like everywhere else across America the treaties were broken. Natives were pressured to move to **reservations** (**reserves** in Canada). Today, many of the 15,000 to 20,000 Northwest Coast People in the United States live on or near reservations. Of about 100,000 Northwest Coast People in British Columbia, perhaps half live on reserves.

The Northwest Coast People had not built their splendid canoes for almost 90 years. But when Washington State began planning a 1989 **centennial** celebration, some tribes proposed a Native Canoe Project. Groups such as the Tulalip, the Quileute [quil-oot], and the Quinault [quin-alt] began to research canoe building. They got special permits to cut ancient cedar trees. On July 21, 1989, 40 dugout canoes representing many tribes arrived in Puget Sound. Dressed in traditional clothing, the participants demonstrated that their history is a vital part of their lives.

The groups that moved onto reservations found the change very difficult. For most of them, salmon was their most important food. Natives lost important fishing grounds in the early 1900s when the government built dams on the Columbia River. Having to live on reservations and take jobs in the community broke up many close-knit families and groups that were accustomed to fishing and working together.

These days, many Northwest Coast People live in houses, drive cars, watch television, and eat many of the same foods that other Americans eat. Children go to public schools and their parents work at a variety of jobs. But to maintain the family cooperation and closeness they once had, families still come together for **powwows**, and they try to take time off from jobs and schools to attend these gatherings.

Traditional Tlingit canoe made of carved and painted wood and metal

Tlingit dancer wearing bear headdress

Humpback whale

Although the sizes and shapes of reservations have changed over the years, one thing is generally true. Each U.S. reservation has its own government with a **sovereign nation** status. The residents have their own laws and tribal organizations, and in many ways are not subject to U.S. or state laws. For example, many reservations have built gambling **casinos** in states where gambling is otherwise illegal. The casinos create jobs and provide money for schools and other programs to raise the standard of living.

Canadian Native groups are called **First Nations**. Many First Nations have turned to tourist activities for income, such as taking visitors whale watching or fishing. Tourism is an industry that can help pay for education, tribal improvements, and social programs.

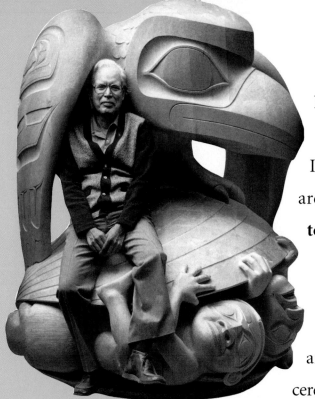

Bill Reid

Bill Reid (1920-1998), Haida artist, taught Native People to look to their heritage for artistic inspiration. He trained as a jeweler, working in gold and silver, and later became a sculptor. He carved red cedar and other woods into canoes, totem poles, and art objects. Reid's 20-foot (6 m) long bronze sculpture, "The Spirit of Haida Gwaii," sits in Vancouver International Airport. It is a green canoe holding mythic figures such as Wolf and Raven. A black version is at the Canadian Embassy in Washington, D.C. Canada named Reid a "National Living Treasure" during his lifetime.

Wherever they live, Native peoples are preserving their heritage. In the most northern areas, they still carve **totem poles** and other objects. They make traditional clothing, baskets, and masks, and practice their ceremonies. Young people study tribal languages, songs, dances, and crafts such as woodcarving. Through storytelling, singing, dancing, and drumming, Northwest Coast People are keeping their history alive.

Native Americans have produced a number of individuals who are outstanding in art, music, film, writing, teaching, and other fields. By listening to their voices, Natives and non-Natives alike can gain greater understanding of the Northwest Coast People–who they once were and who they are today.

Carved animal totem

Chapter II:

WHERE THEY CAME FROM

◄ BERING STRAIT

Scientists believe that Native Americans descended from Asian people who walked across land or ice bridges beginning perhaps 30,000 years ago. It is also possible that some came by boat. A land **migration** would have occurred at the Bering Strait, a narrow waterway between Siberia (a part of Russia) and the present state of Alaska. Sea levels might have been lower then, exposing land.

At the time, ice covered the Northwest Coast region, so these **migrants** moved onto the central plains. Within a few thousand years, their descendants had spread across North, Central, and South America. They divided into hundreds of different groups, speaking many languages. In some areas, they hunted huge **mammoths** and other great animals that are now extinct. Some groups lived as **nomads**, wandering great distances in search of food.

By about 8500 BC, some bands had found their way westward through the high mountain passes and settled along the heavily forested coastline. By 8000 BC, groups were also arriving in large **dugout** canoes. These settlers became the Northwest Coast People.

Clams

What Do the Northwest Coast People Believe about Their Origins?

The creation stories told by a tribe or a nation attempt to explain how people and everything else on Earth came into existence. Most Native tribes believed that the first parents came either from underground or from the sky. But some Northwest Coast groups believe that people emerged from the ocean or from a creature associated with it.

For example, the Haida tell how Raven was on the shore and saw a clam. Its shell was partly open. Raven peeked inside the clamshell and saw a tiny face peeking out. "Come out!" said Raven, who was lonely. A group of tiny people climbed out of the clamshell. These were the first Haida People.

Vancouver Island,
British Columbia, Canada

(Below) raven and (right) illustration of a thunderbird

According to another Haida legend, the universe was divided into three zones–the underworld, the flat earth, and the sky world. People emerged from the underworld, which was ruled by the **orca**, or killer whale. The sky world was ruled by the **thunderbird**. The earth was supported on a cedar pole that was held up by "The Sacred One Standing and Moving."

Orca, or killer whale

Stone harpoon point

The Kwakiutl [kwa-ki-you-tal] and other northern groups believed that animals, which lived on Earth before humans, were very powerful. They spoke to groups of people and transferred some of their powers to them. That is why these groups have clans named after animals. Killer Whale, Grizzly Bear, Eagle, Raven, and Wolf are the names of some of these clans.

Group of Qagyuhl masked dancers and costumed performers in the winter ceremony. The chief stands at the left, grasping a speaker's staff and wearing cedar-bark neck-ring and headband.

A Snohomish legend says that the "Creator and Changer" came from the East, making groups of people and giving them different languages. When he saw Puget Sound, he liked it so much that he scattered the rest of his languages there. That is why there are so many different languages. But he made the sky so low that people bumped their heads. Finally, it was decided that if everyone could communicate by saying "Ya-hoh" ("push together"), they could push the sky up. They cut giant trees and pushed on them to raise the sky. Now, the sky is high enough that people no longer bump their heads on it.

These are just a few among the countless tales that the Northwest Coast People pass from generation to generation to make sure that their history, ancient knowledge, and culture survive.

Haida dancing mask made of carved wood

Chapter III:

LIFE ON THE NORTHWEST COAST

*F*or many centuries, Northwest Coast People had all they could eat. Rivers teemed with **spawning** fish such as salmon, halibut, cod, and smelt. The ocean offered clams, mussels, octopus, seals, whales, and many species of fish. Northwest Coast groups have fished and hunted from boats for centuries. Before restrictions were placed on killing sea mammals, they hunted seals, sea otters, sea lions, **orcas**, gray and humpback whales, and dolphins. Inland, deer, elk, mountain goat, and other game were plentiful, along with many varieties of berries and plants.

The earliest peoples lived in small groups, moving with the seasons but building permanent settlements near the ocean, where they could gather food year-round. By 3000 BC, Natives had harvested so many shellfish that huge piles of shells, or **middens**, appeared. These can still be seen today.

Clayoquot man fishing for flounder and flatfish on the ocean bottom

20

Doctor's dance wand made of carved wood, vegetable pigment, and fur

Because the Northwest Coast People had plenty to eat and year-round shelter, they did not need to move from place to place. They had time to develop a complex culture and advanced artistic skills. The Tlingit, Tsimshian, Haida, Kwakuitl, Nootka, and related peoples of what is now British Columbia made homes, canoes, chests, cradles, clubs, and many other objects out of red cedar. These groups developed expertise in woodcarving and decoration. For centuries, they used sharpened shell, rock, or antler tools to carve the cedar posts supporting their homes.

Elk horn knife

Clamshells

Chipped stone spear point

The carvings represented each family's **totem**, or sacred emblem. Each clan told stories about the origin of its totem. During ceremonies, each chief wore an elaborately carved wooden headdress, bearing the likeness of his totem.

When they acquired metal and could make sharper tools, the northern groups began to carve freestanding totem poles. The size and beauty of the totem poles guarding each home indicated the social status of the family that lived there.

The cedar homes of these northern clans held several families. People slept on raised platforms, with **partitions** for privacy. The only openings in a house were the door and a smoke hole in the roof. In the summer, many boatloads of fish were spread on the roof to dry. In addition, fish hung from 25-foot (7.6 m) tall drying racks beside the house.

These two columns at the Nimkish village at Alert Bay represent the owner's paternal crest, an eagle, and his maternal crest, a grizzly bear.

These peoples wove beautiful baskets, and some groups carved platters and other objects out of shell or stone. Because they made and collected these articles in large numbers, they found ways of displaying their wealth. They invented a gift-giving ceremony called the "**potlatch**." It comes from a Chinook word, patshatl [pat-shat-tel], meaning "give-away."

The potlatch allowed a chief to show his family's status, or rank. Higher-ranking leaders had the biggest potlatches, with many guests and expensive gifts. Potlatches honored special events, such as the birth of a child or the death of a family member. A long-lasting potlatch with many in attendance brought the clan respect.

People of the Northwest Coast developed advanced artistic societies, and this creativity was on display in many everyday items. (Above) a Salish woven basket made of plant fibers, (left) a modern carved totem pole, and (right) a Haida dish box made of wood and metal

Dozens of other groups lived around Puget Sound, along the coastline, and at the mouth of the Columbia River. They spoke languages that came from the Salishan, Chinookian, and Athabascan language families. Although they also lived in cedar plank houses, they did not practice woodcarving

Grizzly bear fishing for salmon

and decorating to the extent that northern tribes did. They did not display their wealth in potlatches to the same degree. The salmon was the most important element in their lives. Many of their spiritual practices revolved around the salmon and its migration. In addition, they hunted deer, elk, goat, bear, and smaller game in nearby forests, valleys, and mountains.

Both northern and southern groups built dugout canoes from large cedar logs. Some were one-person canoes and others were 60-foot (18 m) long, ocean-going boats paddled by many. After acquiring cloth from Europeans, some groups fashioned sails for their boats and learned to sail.

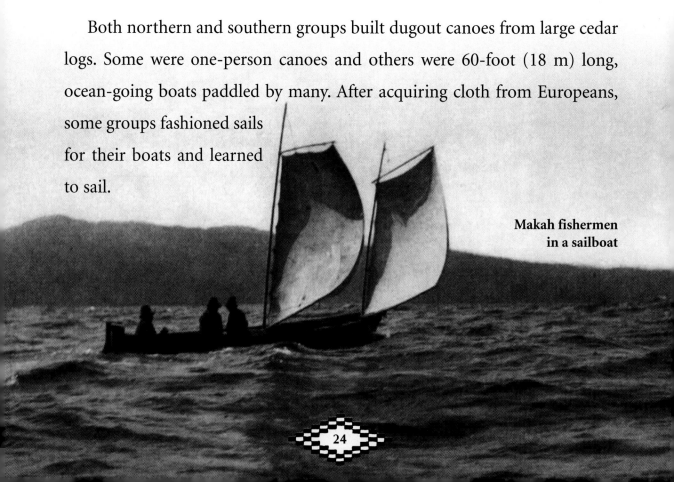

Makah fishermen in a sailboat

All of these peoples knew how to preserve fish by smoking and drying it. To catch the spawning salmon in rivers, they built wooden **weirs**, or gates, and then speared the fish with bone-tipped harpoons. In the tidal zone, they built low stone walls. The fish swam over the wall, only to be trapped when the tide went out.

People used carved wooden clubs to kill fish, sea lions, otters, and even an occasional swimming elk or moose. Whale hunters harpooned 40-ton (36-metric ton) whales from canoes, and hauled them to the beach with rope made of **sinew**. They heated the whale blubber to get oil, ate the meat, and used the intestines to make containers. After about 1910, killing whales was forbidden.

(Above) Native whale hunt

The Makah had not killed a whale since the 1920s because whale populations had fallen. But in 1999, the Makah affirmed their treaty rights to hunt whales. Hunters harpooned a gray whale from canoes and towed it to the beach, where the tribe feasted on meat and blubber. In 2002, the Makah again prepared to hunt, but a panel of judges said they must file environmental impact documents. Animal rights activists applauded the decision, but the Makah prepared to challenge it. They expressed deep concern about the effects of this ruling on fishing rights of all Northwest Native tribes.

Carved wood club

Salish hunters caught ducks and geese with nets made of plant fibers or sinew. They built a small fire on a platform above their canoe stern to attract the ducks at night. When the flock swam close, one man would throw a **dipnet** over it, capturing many. They also netted ducks and seagulls that were feeding on herring eggs in the tidal zone.

Northwest Coast Peoples made baskets, clothing, and hats from woven cedar bark, clubs from yew wood, and drills from bone. Mussel shells became strong harpoon points. Cedar planks were heated and bent to form the seamless corners of watertight storage boxes. Wooden bowls held whale or seal oil for flavoring food. The Makah and nearby tribes wove blankets on wooden **looms** that were inlaid with shells and fish teeth. They wove these blankets from the short, wooly fur of a special kind of dog they raised.

Wishham man fishing with a dipnet. In the pools along the shore the salmon sometimes lie resting.

Woven hats like this would be painted with decorative designs.

Northwest Coast Peoples decorated their clothing and other objects with beautiful designs. Many groups used vegetable dyes to paint elaborate tattoos on their faces and bodies. Northern people wore **nose rings**, made out of bone, and later out of metal. This custom showed peoples' rank and wealth.

Each year, the Northwest Coast People gathered on the Columbia River at a trade fair hosted by the Chinook. Although the groups spoke different languages, they communicated through interpreters and by **sign language**. The Tlingit and Tsimshian paddled great distances, bringing furs, porcupine quills, fish oil, and slaves. Even the peaceful Coastal Salish groups sometimes captured slaves from other bands. They, in turn, had to be alert for slave raids on their villages.

Kwakiutl woman painting a woven grass hat

Some Northwest Coast Tribes

The warlike Tlingit wore helmets made of horns and nose rings. They carved huge ocean-going boats. They had two main clans, the Wolves and the Ravens. The Tlingit experienced change when gold prospectors rushed to Alaska in the 1880s. Some Tlingit went to work in the mines, and others hauled miners' goods in their canoes. But Natives could not file their own mining claims until 1931.

The clothing of this Wishham girl shows the elaborate dress of some Northwest people.

The Haida were some of the first people to make canoes faster by adding sails. From more than 6,000 in 1835, their population is now about 2,000. Most of their ancient villages are abandoned. The Haida still catch and preserve the salmon in the traditional ways and stage salmon festivals, with singing, dancing, feasting, and prayers of thanksgiving. In the 1960s they revived the art of carving totem poles, and in 1989 the Haida celebrated the first new pole rising in 90 years.

Kwakiutl ceremonial dancers representing Wasp, Thunderbird, and Grizzly Bear arrive in ocean-going canoes.

The Kwakiutl occupied the northeast coast of Vancouver Island and the nearby mainland. Subgroups include the Haisla, the Heiltsuk, the Bella Bella, and the Bella Coola. They controlled a channel that is now the Strait of Georgia and sometimes forced other tribes to pay **tribute** before passing through.

The Nootka lived on the southwest edge, or **windward** side, of Vancouver Island. They danced the **Nutlam**, or Wolf Dance, which celebrated an ancient legend about learning survival skills from wolves. They were master canoe builders and whalers. Today they call themselves the "Nuu-chah-nulth speaking First Nations."

Dance of the Eclipsed Moon. It was thought that an eclipse was the result of a creature in the sky trying to swallow the moon. The people danced round a smoldering fire of old clothes and hair. The stench rose to the creature's nostrils, and made him sneeze.

About AD 1580, the village of Ozette on the tip of the Oympic Peninsula was buried by a huge mudslide. The disaster created a "time capsule" that shows how the Makah lived before first European contact. More than 55,000 **artifacts** were recovered in the 1970s from the homes of the Qwidicca-atx [kwid-ick-ah-ax], or "People Who Live on the Cape by the Rocks and Seagulls." Some of these artifacts are displayed at the Makah Cultural and Research Center, along with replicas of cedar houses and canoes.

Whale Hunter, member of the Makah people

About 1,000 Makah [ma-ka], meaning "Cape people," live at Neah Bay on Washington's Olympic Peninsula. Besides fishing and gathering plants, they once hunted whales. Whaling was dangerous and commanded the highest respect. Only chiefs and their relatives could be whalers. The Makah were moved to a small reservation in 1893, but after World War II, their descendants bought an abandoned Army camp and created their own reservation. Recently, they have revived many traditions, teaching their language and crafts and celebrating their heritage through song and dance.

The Quinault [kwin-alt], a large Salish group on the Olympic Peninsula, lived in cedar houses. The Quinault Indian Nation remained in its original homeland, and in 1974 they developed a model forestry program, aided by private industry, government, and universities. Now, their forests are their greatest economic resource. Also, they have restored their coastline and offer guided tours and fishing.

Many Coastal Salish groups lived on the shores of Puget Sound. The Salish included the Skagit, Skokomish, Snohomish, Songish, Snoqualmi, Squamish, Stillaguamish, Twana, Wynochee, and many others. Most groups have either disappeared or merged with larger clans such as the Muckleshoot, Lummi, or Puyallup [pew-al-up].

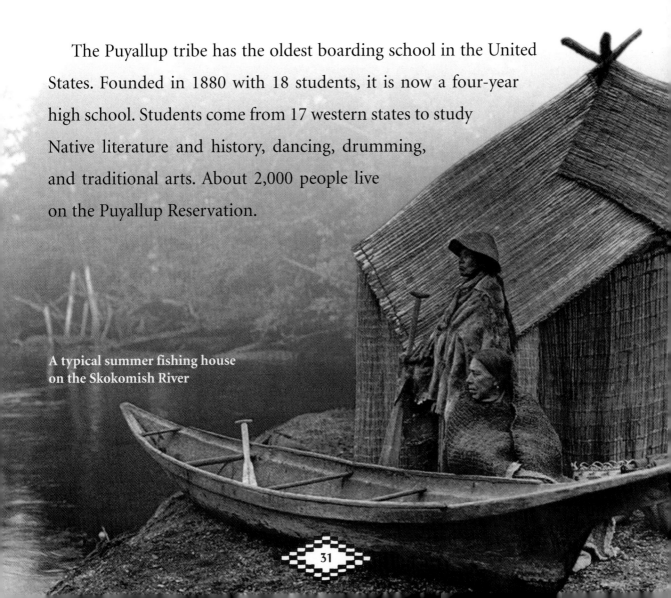

The Puyallup tribe has the oldest boarding school in the United States. Founded in 1880 with 18 students, it is now a four-year high school. Students come from 17 western states to study Native literature and history, dancing, drumming, and traditional arts. About 2,000 people live on the Puyallup Reservation.

A typical summer fishing house on the Skokomish River

Engraving made by A. T. Agate in 1841 of Chinook group inside a cedar plank lodge. There is a pot over a fire and fish drying on racks over the fire pit.

A number of Salish bands merged to form the Muckleshoot. The reservation's name came from Muckleshoot Prairie, near Auburn, Washington. Its residents had lived along rivers and learned to use **cattails** in many ways. They wove them into mats for partitions in houses, door coverings, clothing, mattresses, and pillows. About 3,300 Muckleshoot live on or near the reservation and operate a successful casino.

The Chinook built plank houses around the mouth of the Columbia River and had trading relationships with other tribes. Salmon was their chief livelihood and food. In 1806, they met the Lewis and Clark expedition in elaborately carved and decorated canoes. Today, perhaps 1,000 of the various Chinook bands live on the Grand Ronde, Warm Springs, and Yakima reservations in Oregon and Washington.

Chapter IV:

WHAT THEY BELIEVE

*A*ll Native peoples' calendars, religion, and legends are based on nature. Their lives once depended entirely upon the earth and all that grew on it. To them, everything on earth has a spiritual purpose and everything is interconnected. Although they may have adapted to new ways and new religions, the old faith remains alive. Their belief that nature is sacred is evident in their teachings, writings, art, and culture.

The salmon was so important to Northwest Coast Peoples that some tribes have legends about the fish that sacrificed itself to feed humans. Each year, in the First Salmon Ceremony, the Salish honored the first salmon caught on its way to its birthplace. The fish was brought to the village, cooked in a special way, and shared among everyone. Later, its skeleton would be placed in the same river, facing upstream, and asked to tell its fellow salmon about the fine hospitality it had received.

Salmon swimming upstream

Among the southern groups, young people tried to acquire one or more guardian spirits. The spirit, such as an animal, bird, or fish, was key to the person's future and would remain with them for life. If a woman had a female spider as her guardian, she was destined to be a weaver. Often, the spirit came through a special ceremony or a **vision quest**. Boys and girls began to go on vision quests when they were about 10 years old. They would stay in the woods for days, waiting for a message from a spirit. Some Natives continue this tradition today.

A person with great spiritual power might become a **shaman**, or healer. While dreaming or on a vision quest, the shaman acquires unique songs and dances, which have spiritual meaning. Shamans act as "go-betweens" and interpret the spirit world for humans. They cure illness, lead rituals and **ceremonies**, and preside over burials, among other duties. They wear traditional carved wooden masks, representing powerful animal spirits.

Drums and drumming represent the pulse of the universe and the human heartbeat. Northern tribes suspended wooden box drums from the ceiling and beat them with their hands, which were covered with shredded cedar bark. Shamans used deerskin-covered **tambourine** drums. Winter dances celebrated each clan's spiritual legends. Today, both men and women perform traditional dances at powwows and winter ceremonies.

Nootka man

"All things are connected. Whatever befalls the earth befalls the children of the earth." —Chief Seattle

Early Native peoples could not understand the European view that the earth is something that can be bought and sold. When settlers cut down forests for houses, plowed the earth to plant crops, and fenced the land to keep others out, Natives were shocked. These actions struck deeply at their belief that the earth is sacred.

Once, the survival of Native tribes depended on having strong and brave warriors, so warriors' deeds were honored through ceremonies. Today, that feeling is kept alive in the respect shown to veterans of U.S. wars. Large numbers of Native men and women have served in the Armed Forces. Native Americans have fought for the United States in every war. Today, powwows and tribal ceremonies often include flag songs and similar observances for Native veterans.

Chapter V:

THE ARCTIC AND SUBARCTIC PEOPLES

*N*orth of the Northwest Coast Region, two other Native North American cultures have thrived in a vast, largely inhospitable realm. These are the Arctic and Subarctic Peoples.

The Aleut [a-loot] and the Inuit [in-yoo-it], otherwise known as the Eskimo, inhabit the Arctic Region. Their domain extends for more than 5,000 miles (8,047 km), from the Aleutian Islands to the coast of Greenland. It includes most of Alaska and north central Canada. The Arctic Peoples were probably the last wave of migrants to cross from Siberia between 6000 and 2000 BC.

A family of Eskimos

The Subarctic Peoples generally speak languages from the Northern Athabascan, or Dené ("the people"), and the Algonkian families. Their homeland is huge, containing much of present-day Canada and a section of interior Alaska. The Athabascan groups probably migrated from Siberia between 9000 and 5000 BC. They have a distant relationship with the Apache and Navajo of the Southwest. Most of the Algonkian-speaking tribes came up from the Northeast Woodlands in the 17th and 18th centuries, drawn by the fur trade.

The climate in both regions is harsh, with six-week-long summers and long, extremely cold winters. Temperatures below -40° F (-15° C) and fierce, icy storms are common. For nearly six months in winter, the sun does not rise in the most northern sections. These conditions would seem to make survival impossible. Nevertheless, dozens of communities have flourished throughout this land for centuries.

Homes at King Island, Alaska

The Arctic People

In the Arctic, perhaps 60,000 Aleut and Inuit once lived. Today, there are about 2,500 Aleut and 45,000 Inuit. The Aleut occupy the Aleutian Islands, which extend southwestward in a long chain from Alaska. Most of the Inuit ("the people") live in Nunavut, the northern and eastern section of the Northwest Territories. They were given the name Eskimo ("raw flesh eaters") by the Algonkian-speaking peoples to the south.

These people depended almost completely on the sea. By 100 BC, whaling was a dominant occupation. They also ate fish, seals and sea lions, **caribou**, moose, and smaller game. The Aleut hunted the sea otter for its fur, which became a main attraction for Europeans in the 18th century (see Chapter I).

Eskimos in kayaks at Noatak, Alaska, in 1929

The Inuit hunted from 12-man canoes or one-person kayaks made of wood covered with seal, whale, or walrus hide. Some northern groups used dogs to carry burdens. When Europeans introduced larger dogs, they developed the **dogsled**, which had wooden runners and was pulled by dogs in harness. The Inuit spent winters in coastal areas, fishing through holes in the ice and hunting seal. In spring, they migrated inland to spend their summers following caribou.

The Inuit of Northern Canada lived in dome-shaped **igloos** made of blocks of compacted snow in the winter. Elsewhere, their winter home was the **karmat**, a semi-buried hut of wood or whalebone covered with sod. In summer, all groups moved to skin-covered lodges. Some tribes on Prince William Sound, Alaska, built wooden slab houses that were similar to Tlingit homes.

Both men and women traditionally wore sealskin parkas, hoods, leggings, and boots. Sealskin is ideal for this climate–windproof, waterproof, and warm. Seal or walrus gut was used for parkas and mittens. Caribou skins have been widely used for parkas and hoods, while trousers were sometimes made of polar bear or moleskin. Although the Inuit and Aleut today wear modern clothing, they continue to make weatherproof garments from fur and skins. Parka hoods are often large enough to hold a baby.

Eskimo goggles made of wood helped protect the eyes.

Until about 150 years ago, the Inuit made wooden long-billed hats that shielded their faces from both sun and storms while hunting. They were often decorated with **ivory** carvings from walrus tusks. The Inuit also wore snow goggles made of wood or bone to protect their eyes from the glare of snow and ice.

Unlike other widely scattered peoples, the Inuit did not develop numerous languages. People across the entire Arctic Region can talk together in their native tongue, called **Inuktitut**. They also share beliefs. For instance, Sedna, the Sea Mother, is familiar to most northern peoples. She is the one who symbolically controls the sea's movements and the migration of fish and seals.

Sails were extremely useful in the island climate of the Alaskan Eskimo.

The Subarctic People

The land of the Subarctic People ranges from heavily forested high mountains to swampy **tundra**. Like the Northwest Coast People, they made houses, canoes, cradles, bows, and many other necessary items from cedar, birch, and other types of wood. They excelled in decorating clothing with porcupine quills and animal hair and later with beadwork.

Today, the largest groups of the Athabascan-speaking peoples are the Koyukon near the Yukon River; the Kutchin, to the east; the Carrier in northern British Columbia; the Chipewyan, in northern British Columbia, Alberta, and Manitoba; and the Slavey, mostly in the Northwest Territories. In addition, two dozen smaller groups are scattered throughout the western half of the region.

The Algonkian-speaking tribes dominate the eastern Subarctic Region. Many have names that come from French. Some of the first Europeans to arrive in present-day Canada and the United States were French trappers. Thus, the French changed the tribal name Kenistenoag to "Kristineaux" [kristin-oh], and that name evolved into a short form, "Cree." Subgroups of the Cree include the Plains Cree in the United States and the West Main Cree and Western Woods Cree in Canada.

North Fork Pass, Yukon, Canada

Many tribes made harpoons by attaching a spear tip to a handle often made of bone or wood. Tips were first made of stone or shell and later of metal acquired through trade.

Because of early contact with Europeans, by the 18th century Algonkian-speaking peoples were dependent on European goods such as guns, metal traps, and canvas tents. But they continued to build spruce and skin houses, birchbark canoes, and native snares. They lived among numerous lakes, rivers, and streams, and they were adept hunters and fishermen. Some groups killed seals with **harpoons**, traveling inland in summer to hunt caribou, moose, and deer. They used **toboggans** and dogsleds to travel across snow and ice.

These people probably numbered several hundred thousand at one time. Today, about 140,000 remain. Many have moved to cities such as Winnipeg, but others live on reserves in the **provinces** of Labrador, Quebec, Ontario, and west into Alberta.

Old Eskimo dog team at Indian Point, Siberia in Russia

Eskimos setting out from their island home, the Asiatic coast visible in the background

Arctic and Subarctic Peoples have sometimes succeeded in getting laws passed that protect their rights. For example, in 1945, the Territory of Alaska passed a landmark Anti-discrimination Act. In 1966, the Alaska Federation of Natives was established. In 1994, the Inuit and Aleut published the Alaskan Natives Commission Report, the first major public study of Natives done by Natives. However, the fight to keep traditional fishing and hunting rights continues. In the United States, the Marine Mammal Protection Act of 1972 made it much harder for Alaskan Natives to hunt seals and sea lions as they once did.

In Canada, especially in provinces with large First Nation populations, Native languages are taught in schools and officially recognized. More than 25 percent of First Nation Peoples are **fluent** in their original languages.

These are just some of the ways in which Arctic and Subarctic Peoples are affirming their heritage and keeping their cultures alive. Modern technology such as the Internet is also helping groups communicate among their widely scattered members and preserve their history.

Sea lions on the beach

A TIMELINE OF THE HISTORY OF THE NORTHWEST COAST PEOPLE

30,000 to 13,000 BC - Ice ages lower sea levels, making it possible for people to walk across a land bridge from Asia to North America

12,000 to 9000 BC - Earth warms up and the ice caps melt, allowing people to move throughout North, Central, and South America.

9000 to 5000 BC - Athabascan groups migrate from Siberia to the New World.

6000 to 2000 BC - The Arctic Peoples migrate from Siberia.

100 BC - Whaling has become a dominant occupation.

AD 1492 - Christopher Columbus arrives in America.

AD 1660 to 1800 - Algonkian-speaking tribes migrate from the Northeast Woodlands, drawn by the fur trade.

AD 1741 to 1800 - Russian traders force the Aleut to hunt sea otter for the fur market in China.

AD 1750s - England's Northwest Company and Hudson Bay Company send traders into this region seeking furs.

AD 1776 - The American Revolution, formation of the United States of America.

AD 1778 - James Cook reaches Vancouver Island.

AD 1806 - The Chinook meet the Lewis and Clark Expedition.

AD 1840 to 1870 - The independent nation of Canada, a member of the British Commonwealth, begins to form and acquire land, uniting English-speaking and French-speaking sections.

AD 1846 - The boundary between the United States and Canada is fixed.

AD 1848 - The Oregon Territory is created and settlers begin to move west on the Oregon Trail.

AD 1850 - The Oregon Donation Land Act gives 320 acres (129.5 ha) to each European settler over 18 years old.

AD 1859 - Oregon becomes a U.S. state.

AD 1861 to 1865 - The American Civil War; ends with the abolition of slavery.

AD 1862 to 1885 - Smallpox epidemics kill many Natives.

AD 1871 - British Columbia becomes a Canadian province.

AD 1850s to 1880s - Gold is discovered in British Columbia and Alaska.

AD 1889 - Washington becomes a U.S. state.

AD 1948 - Newfoundland becomes Canada's 10th province.

AD 1959 - Alaska becomes a U.S. state.

GLOSSARY

American Indian - A member of the first peoples of North America.

argillite - A compact clay-like rock cemented by silica.

artifact - Something created by humans, usually an object from long ago.

caribou - A large deer that ranges widely in cold climates; reindeer.

casinos - Buildings used for gambling.

cattail - A tall, reedy marsh plant with brown furry spikes and long, flat leaves.

centennial - The 100th anniversary of something, or the celebration of that anniversary.

ceremony - A formal act or series of acts.

clan - A group of people with a common ancestor or which behaves as a family.

dipnet - A bag net with a handle, used to scoop fish from the water.

dogsled - A vehicle on runners, drawn by dogs.

dugout - A boat made by hollowing out a large log.

First Nations - The Canadian term for Native Americans or American Indians.

fluent - Able to speak and understand easily.

harpoon - A barbed spear used especially in hunting large fish or sea mammals.

Hudson's Bay Company - An English commercial company formed in 1670 to develop business, especially in fur and skins, in the New World.

igloo - A dome-shaped Eskimo (Inuit) house made of blocks of compressed snow or ice.

inlet - A bay or recess in the shore of a sea, lake, or river.

Inuktitut - The language of the Inuit.

ivory - The hard, creamy-white material that composes the tusks of a tusked mammal.

karmat - In Inuktitut, a semi-buried hut of wood or whalebone covered with sod.

language family - A group of languages related to each other by similarities in vocabulary, grammar, and pronunciation.

loom - A frame for weaving threads or yarns to form cloth.

mammoth - Extinct hairy elephants living about 1,600,000 years ago.

midden - A pile of objects, such as bones or shells, that have been gathered.

migrant - A person who moves from one country or place to another.

migration - The movement of a person or group from one country or place to another.

Native American - A synonym for American Indian.

nomad - A person who moves from place to place.

Northwest Company - A commercial company from England that ranged across Canada and into the United States seeking furs and skins.

nose rings - Rings of bone, ivory, metal, or wood puncturing the soft skin or cartilage of the nose, worn as a decoration.

Nutlam - Nootka name of a dance that celebrated a legend about people learning survival skills from wolves.

orca - A black and white dolphin-like type of whale, sometimes called "killer whale."

Oregon Trail - The route from Independence, Missouri, to the Columbia River region.

partition - Something that divides, for example an interior dividing wall.

potlatch - A ceremonial feast of the Northwest Coast people for the purpose of giving lavish gifts and showing off wealth.

powwow - Originally referred to a shaman, a vision, or a gathering. Now, it means a cultural, social, spiritual gathering.

province - A division of a country. Canada has provinces rather than states.

reservation - A tract of public land set aside for a specific use.

reserve - Canadian term for "reservation."

shaman - Medicine man or woman.

sign language - A formal language that uses hand gestures instead of words.

sinew - Fiber from tendons; the animal tissue that connects muscles.

sovereign nation - A community that has independent power and freedom.

spawn - To produce eggs, usually said of fish.

tambourine - A small drum, especially a one-headed drum with metal disks that rattle when the drum is shaken.

thunderbird - In Native myth, a bird that causes lightning and thunder.

toboggan - Algonkian word for a flat-bottomed lightweight sled.

totem - Emblem or revered symbol; spiritual patron, usually an animal.

totem pole - A wooden pole that is carved and painted with the spiritual symbols of a family or clan.

treaty - An agreement or arrangement, usually written, made by negotiating.

tribute - A payment by one ruler or nation to another as the price of protection or to show respect or submission; also, a gift or service showing respect.

tundra - A treeless plain with black, mucky soil over permanently frozen soil, characteristic of arctic and subarctic regions.

vision quest - The seeking of a vision, dream, or perception, which will guide a young person for life; an important part of the passage into adulthood.

weir - A fence or enclosure set in a waterway for taking fish.

windward - Facing the direction from which the wind is blowing.

Books of Interest

Boiteau, Denise and David Stansfield. *Early Peoples: A History of Canada.* Markham, Ontario, Canada: Fitzhenry & Whiteside Ltd., 1988.

Connolly, James E., comp. *Why the Possum's Tail is Bare and Other North American Indian Nature Tales.* Owings Mills, Md.: Stemmer House, 1985.

Erlich, Amy, adapter. *Wounded Knee: An Indian History of the American West.* New York: Henry Holt & Co. 1993 (adaptation for young readers of Dee Brown's *Bury My Heart at Wounded Knee,* Henry Holt & Co., 1970).

Erdoes, Richard and Alfonso Ortiz, eds. *American Indian Myths and Legends.* New York: Pantheon, 1984.

Johnson, Michael. *Encyclopedia of Native Tribes of North America.* New York: Gramercy Books, 2001.

La Farge, Oliver. *The American Indian.* New York: Golden Press, 1956.

Nerburn, Kent, ed. *The Wisdom of the Native Americans.* Novato, Calif.: New World Library, 1999.

Woodhead, Henry, series ed. *The American Indians.* Alexandria, Va.: Time Life Inc., 1992-94.

Children's Atlas of Native Americans. Chicago: Rand McNally & Co., 1996.

Good Web Sites to Begin Researching Native Americans

General Information Site with Links
http://www.nativeculture.com

Resources for Indigenous Cultures around the World
http://www.nativeweb.org/

Index of Native American Resources on the Internet
http://www.hanksville.org/NAresources/

News and Information from a Native American Perspective
http://www.indianz.com

An Online Newsletter Celebrating Native America
http://www.turtletrack.org

Native American History in the United States
http://web.uccs.edu/~history/index/nativeam.html

Internet School Library Media Center
http://falcon.jmu.edu/~ramseyil/native.htm

Alaska Federation of Natives
http://www.nativefederation.org

Canada's First Nations
http://www.ainc-inac.gc.ca/

http://www.johnco.com/nativel/

INDEX

Linda Thompson is a Montana native and a graduate of the University of Washington. She has been a teacher, writer, and editor in the San Francisco Bay Area for 30 years and now lives in Taos, New Mexico. She can be contacted through her web site, http://www.highmesaproductions.com